DESIGNER
Cross Stitch
PROJECTS

DESIGNER Cross Stitch PROJECTS

OVER 100 COLORFUL AND CONTEMPORARY PATTERNS

Editors of *CrossStitcher*

Design Originals

an Imprint of Fox Chapel Publishing
www.d-originals.com

Designer Cross Stitch Projects is an original work, first published in 2013 in the United Kingdom by Future Publishing Limited in magazine form under the title *Designer Stitches*. This title is printed and distributed in North America under license. All rights reserved.

ISBN 978-1-57421-721-6

© 2014 by Design Originals, www.d-originals.com, an imprint of Fox Chapel Publishing, 800-457-9112, 1970 Broad Street, East Petersburg, PA 17520.

Printed in China
First printing

Introduction

EMBRACE THE WORLD OF HANDMADE with this bumper collection of fun, fresh cross stitch projects by today's hottest designers. Inspired by current fashion and interiors trends and bursting with color, you're sure to find something here to suit your style. This book is divided into three sections for easy reference: smaller, funky projects that you can stitch just for fun; fantastic gift ideas for friends and family (or to just keep for yourself!); and larger, beautiful pieces that will look sensational in any home. Make a useful bluebird gadget sleeve (page 14), a sophisticated photo frame (page 92), or a gentleman's glasses case (page 62). Or try your hand at a decorative flower pillow (page 102), a retro typewriter design (page 54), or a lifelike beetle (page 22). Whatever your decision, you'll keep coming back to make more! As well as cross stitch patterns, you'll also find detailed step-by-step instructions, so you can transform your stitching into a variety of professional-looking products and accessories. So jump in to the world of stitching, and get used to proudly saying, "Thanks, I made it myself!"

This taxidermy-inspired bug is right on trend

This colorful camera case just oozes retro cool

This nifty gadget cozy keeps your tech stylish and scratch-free

Show off your stitching with this fun tote

Contents

YOU ARE MY SUNSHINE

Turn to page 20 for this cool retro camera case

102

108

HOMESTYLE

Find this super-bright cushion on page 96

Stitching Basics

TOOLS OF THE TRADE

NEEDLES

For basic stitching you'll need a tapestry needle that has a blunt tip and large eye. Use a size 24 needle for most aidas, and a size 26 for evenweaves and linens. Use a sharp embroidery needle for finer details such as backstitch and French knots.

EMBROIDERY SCISSORS

Embroidery scissors are an absolute must-have for stitchers and can be picked up for just a few dollars. Keep yours sharp by only using them to cut threads — that way a decent pair should last you a lifetime.

EMBROIDERY THREAD

Embroidery thread is sometimes referred to as stranded cotton. Each thread length is made up of six strands of cotton twisted together. The chart key will indicate how many strands you'll need to stitch your design with.

HOOPS AND FRAMES

Though not absolutely essential, it is recommend to use an embroidery hoop or frame to keep an even stitching tension. Just make sure it's big enough to fit your entire design.

AIDA

Aida is an ideal choice for cross stitch beginners. 14 count is the most common, although it's available in a huge variety of colors and counts. Each cross stitch is worked over a single aida block, making counting and keeping your place a cinch.

EVENWEAVE

Evenweave is much simpler to work with than you might think. Start with a 26 or 28 count evenweave fabric. Once you're confident, try your hand at a linen version.

THE CHART

START stitching from the center of the design and your fabric. The center of these charts are indicated by dotted lines. To find the center of your fabric, fold it in half and then into quarters.

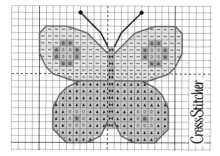

Reading the chart

EACH square on the chart represents a single cross stitch. Fractionals are half filled squares or squares filled with two different colors.

	DMC	Anchor	Madeira
Cross stitch in two strands			
☆	602	057	0611
0	741	314	0202
⋈	3799	236	1713
▲	3839	176	0906
~	3840	120	0907
Backstitch in one strand			
—	3799	236	1713
butterfly antennae			
—	3838	940	0905
all other details			
French knots in two strands			
●	3799	236	1713
butterfly antennae			

THE KEY

ALL THE symbols that appear on the chart are listed in the key with their corresponding thread codes beside them. The key also tells you the different stitches used in the design.

Color match

IN THE key, the closest column of thread codes listed next to the chart symbols is the thread brand that's used in the design. Similar color matches are listed alongside it.

Start stitching... on aida

Step 1

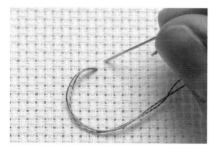

CUT a 15 ¾″ (40cm) thread length, and thread your needle with two of the six strands. Knot one end and start with a waste knot. Make a diagonal half cross stitch across a single aida block.

Step 2

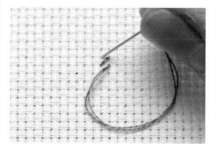

MAKE a second diagonal stitch to complete your first cross. Alternatively, you can work a row of half cross stitches first, then work back on yourself to complete the stitches.

Step 3

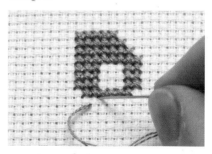

THE direction of your diagonals is up to you; just be sure all your stitches cross in the same direction. Otherwise, your design will look uneven. Continue working from the center outward.

Start stitching... **on evenweave**

Step 1

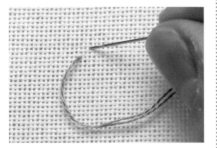

INSTEAD of taking your needle diagonally across a single aida block, take your needle diagonally across two evenweave threads, creating a half cross stitch as before.

Step 2

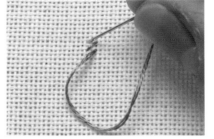

MAKE a second diagonal stitch to complete your first cross stitch. Work each stitch individually or work a row of half cross stitches, then work back on yourself to complete the stitches.

Step 3

CONTINUE working from the center of your design outward. If you find the extra counting a bit daunting at first, don't give up. It'll become second nature in no time.

BACKSTITCH

Use this easy stitch to give a neat outline and add details

Step 1

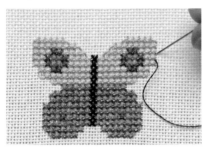

WORK your backstitch using a sharp needle, once you've finished the cross stitch. To secure your thread, weave it through the back of your stitches, then bring your needle up to the surface.

Step 2

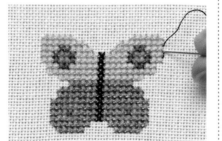

WORK your backstitch over about 1-3 chart squares at a time, making sure to closely follow the chart. Any longer and your stitches could end up becoming loose and pulling out.

Step 3

FOR each additional stitch, bring your needle up 1-3 chart squares away from your previous stitch. Then pass it back through the fabric at the same point as your previous stitch.

FRENCH KNOTS

Go dotty with this simple way to add neat knots to your designs

Step 1

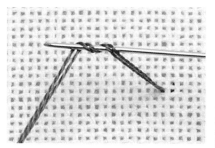

USING a sharp embroidery needle, bring it up at your starting point and wrap your thread once or twice around it. Use one strand for a small knot and two for a slightly chunkier knot.

Step 2

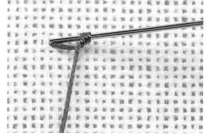

HOLD your thread end firmly and take the needle down, just over from where you came up. Slide the twisted thread down the needle to the fabric's surface, and feed the needle through the fabric.

Step 3

KEEP your thread as taut as possible to prevent the knot becoming loose. Gently pull your thread through to tighten the knot, so that it sits neatly on the surface. Practice will make perfect!

FRACTIONALS

These little stitches are great for adding a bit more detail to your work

Step 1

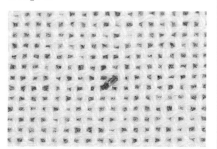

START with a quarter stitch, working from one corner into the center. For evenweave, there is already a hole in the center to stitch into. With aida, you'll need to pierce the center of the block.

Step 2

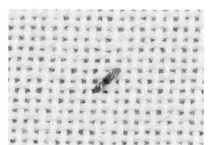

MAKE your next quarter stitch in your second color, coming up from the opposite corner and back down through the center. You've now created a half cross stitch.

Step 3

FINISH your stitch by making a half cross stitch. Fractionals are shown in the chart either as two symbols opposite one another in a chart square, or by a symbol opposite an empty space.

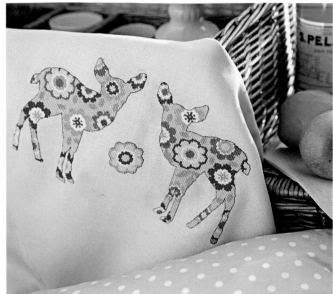

Fun to stitch

Stitch something just because: because it makes you smile, because it's cool and quirky, because it's gorgeous, because it's original, because it's fun!

Designed by: Angela Poole
Design size: 2¾"x3¼" (7x8cm)
Stitch time: 4 hours

MATERIALS

- 14 count waste or soluble canvas, 6½"x6½" (16x16cm)
- Mustard yellow felt
- Metal fasteners

LITTLE BLUEBIRD

Keep your gadgets scratch-free with a beautiful felt cozy in a clashy electric blue and mustard palette

CrossStitcher © Angela Poole

Anchor	DMC	Madeira
Cross stitch in three strands		
0 264	3348	1409
★ 1090	996	1103
Backstitch in one strand		
—— 148	311	1005
all details		
French knots in one strand		
● 148	311	1005
eye		

Make a... gadget cozy

Step 1

ONCE you're done stitching, remove the waste canvas. Cut your felt piece plus a second piece to 3 ½"x6 ½" (9x16cm) or to fit your phone.

Step 2

MAKE about a ¾" (2cm) fold to the reverse along the top edge of each piece. Secure with fabric glue and iron for a crisp edge.

Step 3

PIN your felt pieces together. Add a blanket stitch edge using six strands of Anchor 1090. Add metal fasteners at the top.

How to... blanket stitch

Step 1

BRING your needle up to the front to start stitching. Bring your needle back down just a few millimeters (about a quarter of an inch) away from where you came up.

Step 2

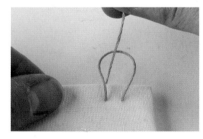

BEFORE pulling your thread all the way through, pass your needle through the thread loop, from back to front, to create your first stitch.

Step 3

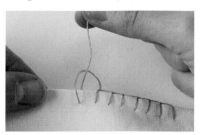

CONTINUE for each additional stitch, taking your needle down through the fabric and passing your needle through the thread loop.

Space invaders

The aliens have landed! Stitch these colorful video game icons on anything you like for an instant splash of retro pop culture

Designed by: Diane Machin **Stitch time:** 1–2 hours each

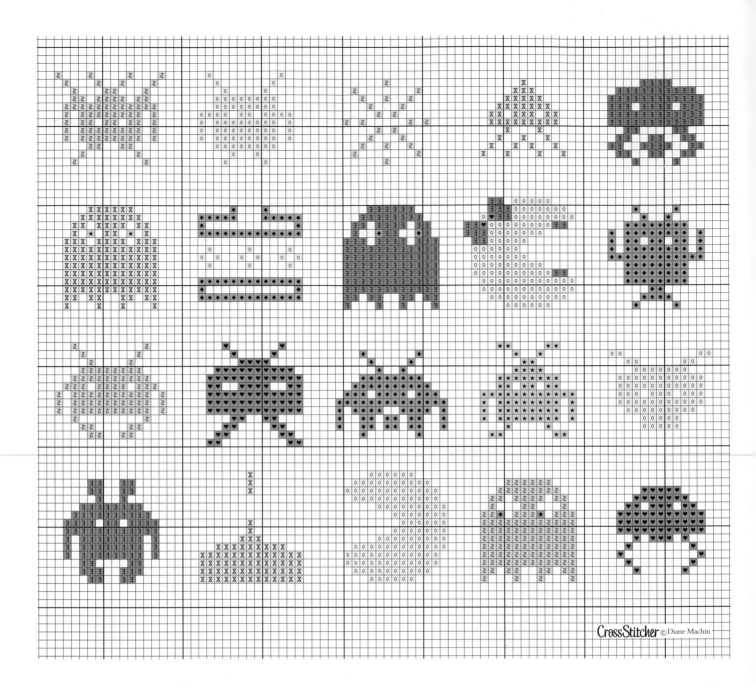

Make a... **covered button**

Step 1

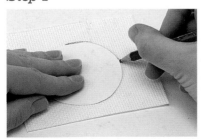

USE the template provided on your self-cover button packaging to cut your fabric into a circle, with your stitching in the middle. Alternatively, simply cut the fabric into a 2 ½″ (6cm) circle.

Step 2

PULL your fabric around the button front as tight as you can. If you like, add a small piece of double-sided tape to both the front and the inside of the button to hold your fabric in place.

Step 3

USE your fingernail to tighten and smooth any lumpy areas around the perimeter of your button. Once you're happy with it, pop the plastic backing securely into place.

A colorful space invader key ring will ensure you always know which set belongs to you

	DMC	Anchor	Madeira
Cross stitch in three strands			
★	702	226	1306
Ǝ	718	088	0707
O	744	301	0112
♥	817	013	0211
X	907	255	1410
S	996	433	1103
♦	3843	1089	1102

MATERIALS

- 14 count colored aida, 4"x4" (10x10cm) piece for each button
- 1⅛" (29mm) self-cover buttons

Designed by: Kerry Morgan
Design size: 3"x5" (7.5x12.5cm) Stitch time: 14 hours

Smile!

Keep your camera safe and smart in this picture-perfect case
for a look that's oozing retro charm. Say cheese!

DMC	Anchor	Madeira
Cross stitch in two strands		
0 White	002	2402
◄ 310	403	2400
@ 318	235	1714
~ 415	398	1802
♥ 891	035	0411
★ 3846	1090	1103
Backstitch in one strand		
—— 310	403	2400
all details		

Not a fan of turquoise? Swap it for your favorite shade!

MATERIALS

- 28 count white evenweave, 11"x13" (28x33cm)
- Turquoise fabric, 6¾"x9" (17x23cm)
- White lining fabric, 6¾"x12¼" (17x31cm)
- Jump rings
- Thin black cord, 1yd (1m)
- Velcro® or metal fasteners

Make a... camera pouch

Step 1

TRIM your stitching ¾" (2cm) beyond the stitched edge. Cut your turquoise fabric to the same width and 9" (23cm) long. Right sides in, machine sew to the top of your stitching.

Step 2

OPEN out and press the seam. Cut white lining fabric the same size. Right sides in, sew the pieces together, leaving an opening. Turn right sides out and slip stitch the opening closed.

Step 3

FOLD into thirds, creating a top flap and pocket. Pin and sew to secure the pocket. Add a jump ring to either side, then loop black cord through. Attach metal fasteners or a Velcro® closure.

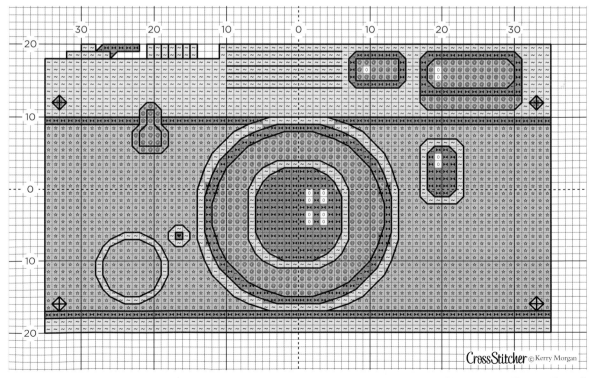

CrossStitcher © Kerry Morgan

Bug-a-boo

A beautiful taxidermy-inspired bug in dazzling shades of green and gold

The craft of taxidermy has been enjoying a revival. Antique animal heads and framed critters have been popping up on the walls of trendy bars, and interesting replicas are even appearing in the newest fashions. Designer Genevieve Brading – AKA Floss & Mischief – began stitching "taxidermy" beetles to placate her partner's desire to have the real deal in their home: "Beetles come in a beautiful array of glowing colors and shapes," says Genevieve. "Cross stitch gives the critters a lovely texture, and metallic thread reflects their jewel-like quality."

Designed by: Floss & Mischief
Design size: 6¼"x8½" (15.5x21.5cm)
Stitch time: 16 hours

Turn to page 27 for a quick guide to mounting your stitched design in an embroidery hoop

Stitch it on aida!
If you'd rather stitch on aida, go for 14 count rustic aida

MATERIALS

- 28 count rustic linen, 17¾"x17¾" (45x45cm)
- 10 inch wooden stitch hoop
- Turquoise paint
- Cream backing fabric
- Cream felt

METALLIC THREADS

Make life easier when working with metallic threads by using beeswax or a thread conditioner. It will strengthen your threads and help them pass more easily through your fabric.

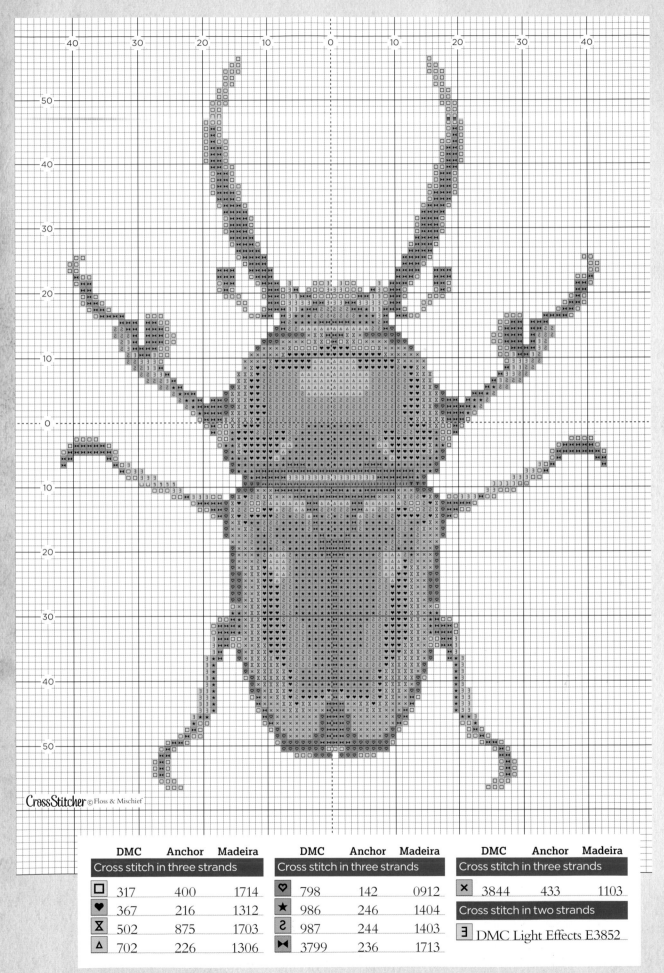

	DMC	Anchor	Madeira
Cross stitch in three strands			
⬜	317	400	1714
♥	367	216	1312
✕	502	875	1703
△	702	226	1306

	DMC	Anchor	Madeira
Cross stitch in three strands			
♥	798	142	0912
★	986	246	1404
ꙅ	987	244	1403
⋈	3799	236	1713

	DMC	Anchor	Madeira
Cross stitch in three strands			
✕	3844	433	1103
Cross stitch in two strands			
Ǝ	DMC Light Effects E3852		

FIRST CLASS

Travel in style with this red, white and blue airmail-inspired passport holder. It's a jet setter must-have!

Designed by: Rebecca Tuffnell
Design size: 4"x5¾" (10x14.5cm)
Stitch time: 7 hours

	DMC	Anchor	Madeira
Cross stitch in two strands			
♥	321	047	0510
△	666	046	0210
~	712	387	2101
◆	825	162	1011
☆	826	161	1012
O	3865	926	2403
Backstitch in one strand			
——	310	403	2400
stamp			
——	321	047	0510
all other details			
——	825	162	1011
arrow, heart, stamp			

Make a...
passport cover

Step 1

TRIM your stitching to ¾″ (1.5cm) beyond the stitched edge, all the way around. Back with a piece of white fabric that's the same size.

Step 2

MACHINE stitch a 7″x7″ (17.5x17.5cm) piece of red polka dot fabric to the left side of your stitching, and a 3 ½″x7″ (8.5x17.5cm) piece to the right side. Open out and press the seams flat. Cut a second piece of patterned fabric to the same size as your sewn piece. Right sides in, pin and machine sew the two pieces together, leaving an opening ready for turning.

Step 3

TURN out and slip stitch the opening closed. Using your passport as a guide, fold the right and left hand sides toward the middle, creating approximately 2″ (5cm) deep pockets. Use some coordinating thread and a sharp needle to hand-sew the top and bottom of the pockets. Be sure to only sew through the lining.

Yes, you can stitch on planes! Needles are fine, but leave your embroidery scissors at home and use a thread cutter instead

MATERIALS

- 28 count white evenweave, 10″x10″ (25x25cm)
- Red polka dot fabric, see step-by-step for sizing
- White fabric, see step-by-step for sizing

RetroDAZE

For a colorful stitch try this deer duo, inspired by
the playful patterns of 1960s and 70s textiles

To make a stitch hoop, first cut your stitching and some backing fabric down into a circle, then mount the pieces into your frame and tighten. Wrap the extra fabric around to the back and secure it down. You have your hoop!

Designed by: Lucie Heaton
Design size: 6¼"x9¾"
(15.5x24.5cm)
Stitch time: 28 hours

MATERIALS

- 28 count cream evenweave, 17¾"x17¾" (45x45cm)
- Wooden embroidery hoop
- Turquoise paint

	DMC	Anchor	Madeira
Cross stitch in three strands			
~	White	002	2402
✕	772	259	1604
♥	892	033	0412
▬	959	186	1113
△	964	185	1112
⊠	3340	329	0301
★	3766	167	1105
Backstitch in one strand			
——	3799	236	1713
	all details		

CrossStitcher © Lucie Heaton

Use these fun alphabet tiles to put together
whatever message you wish – they're perfect
for a quick and simple stitch!

◇◇◇◇◇◇◇◇◇◇◇◇◇◇◇◇◇◇◇◇◇◇◇◇◇◇◇◇◇◇

Designed by: Maria Diaz
Design size: 1½"x1½" (4x4cm) each **Stitch time:** 2.5 hours each

◇◇◇◇◇◇◇◇◇◇◇◇◇◇◇◇◇◇◇◇◇◇◇◇◇◇◇◇◇◇

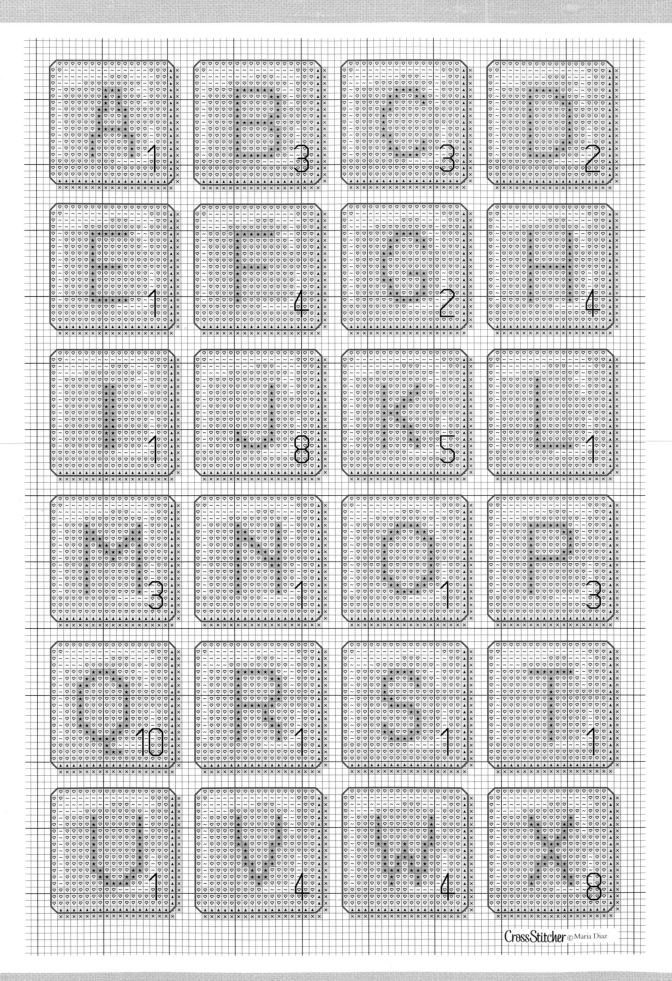

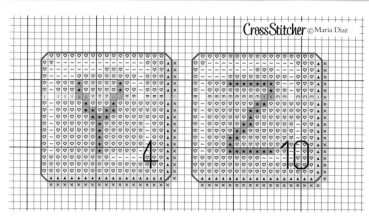

If you're short on time, stitch your tiles on cream felt and skip stitching DMC 677

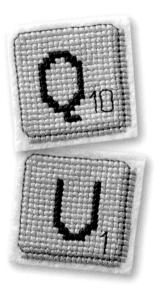

	DMC	Anchor	Madeira
Cross stitch in three strands			
✕	644	391	1814
♥	677	885	2207
~	712	926	2101
▲	738	361	2013
★	844	1041	1809
Backstitch in one strand			
——	310	403	2400
	numbers		
——	646	1040	1812
	tile outlines		

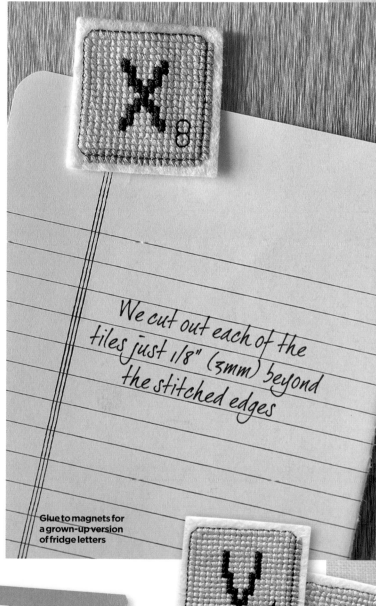

We cut out each of the tiles just 1/8" (3mm) beyond the stitched edges

Glue to magnets for a grown-up version of fridge letters

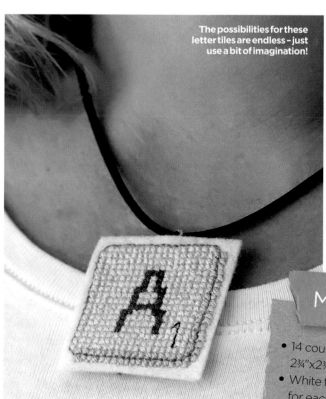

The possibilities for these letter tiles are endless – just use a bit of imagination!

MATERIALS

- 14 count waste or soluble canvas, 2¾"x2¾" (7x7cm) piece for each
- White felt, 2¾"x2¾" (7x7cm) piece for each

MATERIALS

- 28 count rustic linen, 21¼"x23" (54x58cm) piece, two 2½"x23¾" (6x60cm) strips
- Red polka dot fabric, 15"x17" (38x43cm) piece, 3¼"x15" (8x38cm) strip, two 2½"x23¾" (6x60cm) strips
- Cream lining fabric, two 15"x17" (38x43cm) pieces

HOW DO Y●U LIKE
them APPLES?

An apple a day might keep the doctor away, but
this sassy shopper is sure to keep the fashion
police at bay. Golden delicious, anyone?

Designed by: Lucie Heaton
Design size: 9¾"x11¼" (24.5x28.5cm)
Stitch time: 60 hours

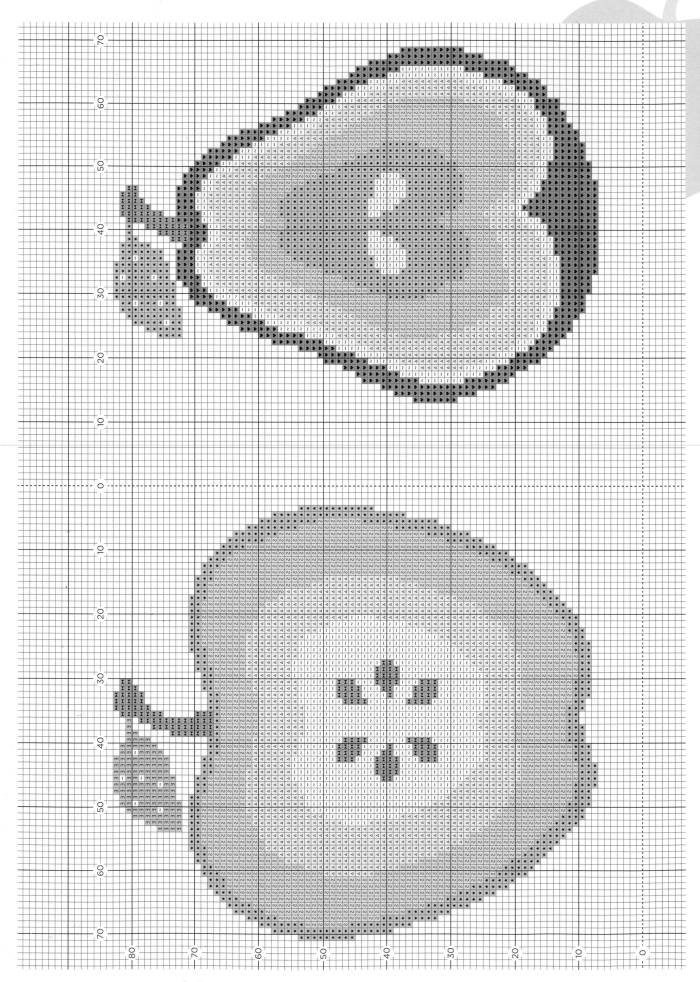

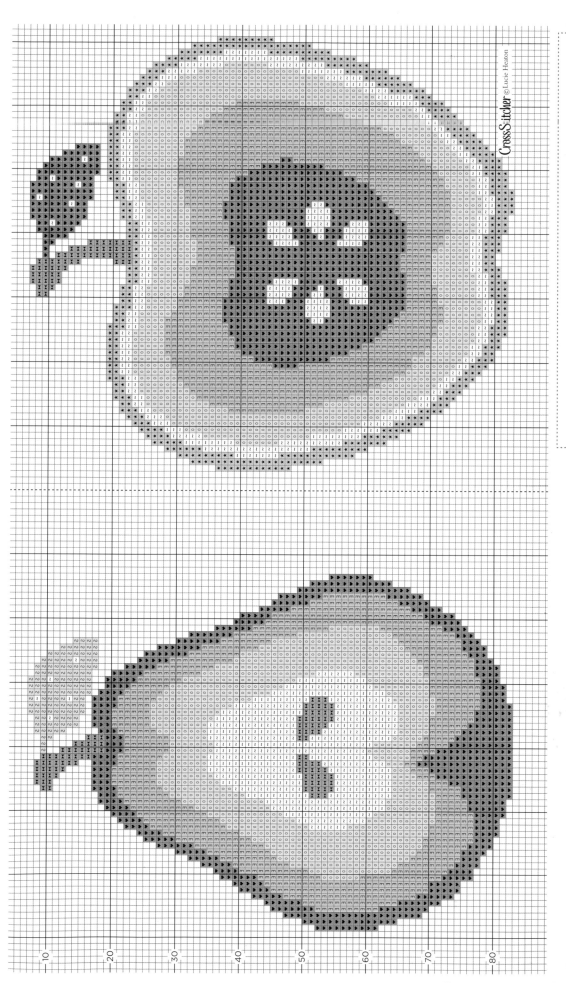

DMC	Anchor	Madeira
Cross stitch in three strands		
★ 702	226	1306
5 704	225	1308
⚊ 839	1086	1913
≀ 3865	926	2403

DMC	Anchor	Madeira
Cross stitch in three strands		
◗ 349	013	0212
⬛ 352	009	0303
○ 353	008	2605
◁ 472	253	1414

CrossStitcher ©Lucie Heaton

Turn to page 52 for a step-by-step guide to making a bag from your stitched linen plus other fabric

The COLOR wheel

Color swatches are a must-have for any artist. Pick your faves from this rainbow wheel!

TANGERINE
DMC 741

FRUIT PUNCH

BLUE
DMC 3843

PACIFIC DREAM

BRICK
DMC 3830

HOT PAPRIKA

MAUVE
DMC 915

RICH BURGUNDY

GREEN
DMC 3850

GEMSTONE JADE

VIOLET
DMC 3746

ULTRA VIOLET

PINK FLAMINGO

MEDITERRANEAN BLUE

ROYAL FLUSH

GREEN ZINGER

EARTHY GLOW

SUMMER SUNSET

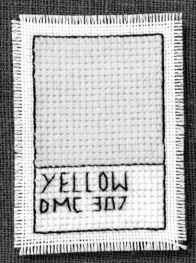

LEMON TWIST

RED CARPET

MULBERRY BUSH

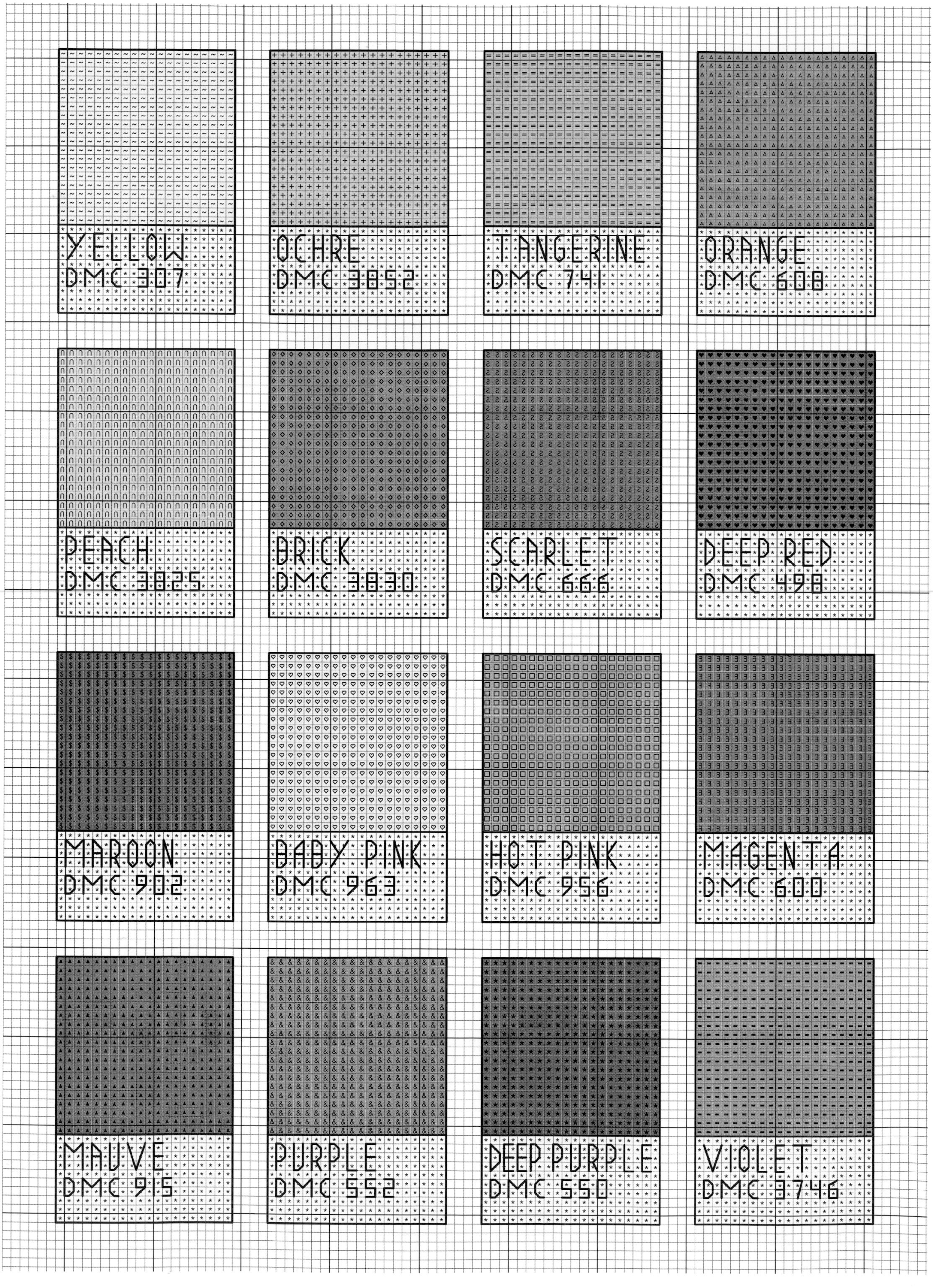

YELLOW
DMC 307

OCHRE
DMC 3852

TANGERINE
DMC 74

ORANGE
DMC 608

PEACH
DMC 3825

BRICK
DMC 3830

SCARLET
DMC 666

DEEP RED
DMC 498

MAROON
DMC 902

BABY PINK
DMC 963

HOT PINK
DMC 956

MAGENTA
DMC 600

MAUVE
DMC 915

PURPLE
DMC 552

DEEP PURPLE
DMC 550

VIOLET
DMC 3746

MATERIALS

- 28 count cream evenweave
- White card for backing

Designed by: Maria Diaz
Stitch time: 3 hours each

DMC	Anchor	Madeira
Cross stitch in two strands		
* B5200	001	2401
~ 307	289	0104
■ 310	403	2400
♥ 498	1005	0511
★ 550	101	0714
& 552	099	0713
Ǝ 600	059	0704
△ 608	330	0205
S 666	046	0210
# 699	923	1303
= 741	304	0203
$ 902	897	0601
× 907	255	1410
▲ 915	1029	0705
□ 956	040	0611
♡ 963	023	0503
o 3364	261	1603
– 3746	1030	2702
∩ 3825	323	2307
◇ 3830	5975	0401
/ 3840	120	0907
◆ 3843	1089	1102
☆ 3844	410	2506
@ 3845	433	1103
▶◀ 3850	189	1203
+ 3852	307	2509
Backstitch in one strand		
—— 310	403	2400
all details		

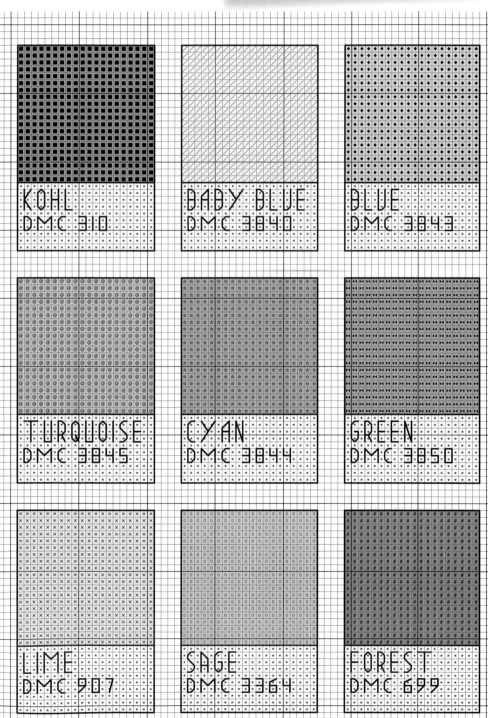

CrossStitcher © Maria Diaz

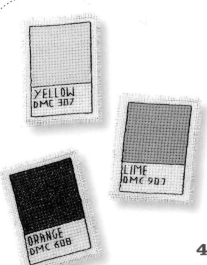

41

Gifts to give

Make someone's day with a stylish gift that's stitched with love – pick from cushions, cozies, totes, sewing kits and all kinds of accessories.

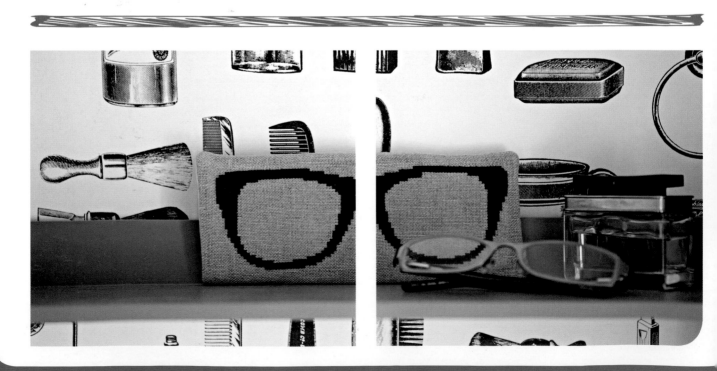

MATERIALS

Tea Cozy
- 26 count evenweave, 13"x13" (33x33cm)
- Patterned fabric, 10¾"x12" (27x30cm)
- Contrasting fabric, 2½"x21¾" (6x55cm) strip
- Lining fabric, two 10¾"x12" (27x30cm) pieces
- Batting, two 10¾"x12" (27x30cm) pieces
- Chunky pink ric rac, 1yd (1m)

If you don't want to create a cozy, turn your design into a framed picture instead!

Funky teatime

Ditch the pastels and chintzy florals – make your mom smile with a riot of vivid color, bold pattern and standout graphics. Tea time just got funky!

Project by: Emily Peacock **Stitch time:** 30 hours

Customize the design to suit your taste by playing with the colors and patterns a bit. For instance, the lettering on the tea cozy shown is in just one thread shade instead of in stripes

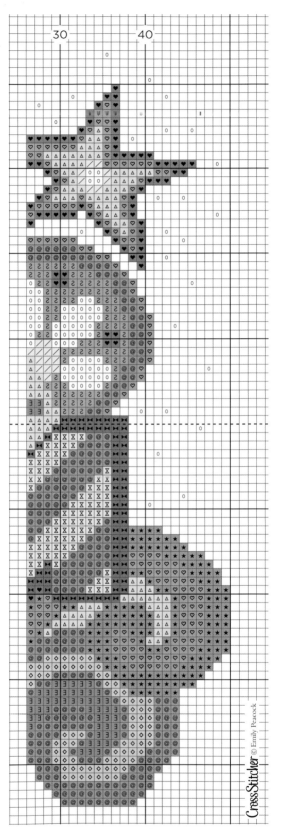

	DMC	Anchor	Madeira
Cross stitch in three strands			
0	White	002	2402
∩	445	288	0103
★	552	099	0713
♡	602	057	0702
@	700	228	1304
◇	742	303	0114
Ⴈ	817	013	0211
X	907	255	1410
♥	917	089	0706
ς	947	330	0205
/	973	290	0105
△	3708	031	0408
⋈	3777	1015	2502

© Emily Peacock

MATERIALS

Framed Picture
- 32 count rustic linen, 13"x13" (33x33cm)
- White painted frame

Make a... **tea cozy**

With this zingy accessory on the table, afternoon tea will never be dull again!

Step 1

CUT two pieces of patterned fabric, two lining, and two batting into half circles. Cut your design to an oval. Sew onto one of your fabric pieces and add ric rac.

Step 2

WITH right sides out, sandwich one piece of batting between your stitched piece and a lining piece. Repeat with the second pieces of fabric, lining and batting.

Step 3

WITH right sides in, pin and stitch the two sets of fabric together, just around the curved edge. Sandwich ric rac between the layers and a fabric tab at the top.

Step 4

FOLD both edges of your fabric strip under and press in place. Now fold the entire strip in half and press again. Wrap around the raw fabric edges and stitch in place.

QUICK STITCH

For a quick alternative, pick up a funky ready made tea cozy. Add your design as a patch and add chunky ric rac just as shown for the perfect finishing touch. No one will know you didn't sew it all yourself!

Shake your TAIL FEATHER

When it comes to feathers, the peacock certainly knows how to shine, and this stunning bag and purse duo will have your recipient dressed to impress

Designed by: Felicity Hall
Design size: 10"x12" (25.5x30cm)
Stitch time: 45 hours

DMC	Anchor	Madeira
Cross stitch in one strand		
○	Kreinik (#8) fine braid 002	
Backstitch in one strand		
—	Kreinik (#8) fine braid 002 all details	

DMC	Anchor	Madeira
Cross stitch in three strands		
★	796	133	0913
◇	907	255	1410
#	913	204	1212
✕	3846	1090	1103

MATERIALS

Bag

- 28 count gray linen, 17¾"x19¾" (45x50cm),
  plus a 11¼"x13" (28.5x33cm) piece for the backing and two 2¾"x21¼" (7x54cm) strips
- Green lining fabric, two 11¼"x13" (28.5x33cm) pieces, two 2¾"x21¼" (7x54cm) strips

Make a... bag

Step 1

TRIM your stitching, backing and lining pieces to 11¼"x13" (28.5x33cm). To create the handles, stitch one linen and one green fabric strip together. Turn out, press and repeat for the other handle.

Step 2

PIN and sew your stitched piece and one lining piece together along the top edge only, sandwiching one of your handles between the layers. Repeat for your remaining pieces.

Step 3

OPEN both pieces out and pin, right sides in, lining up the seams at the middle. Sew around, leaving an opening for turning. Turn right sides out, slip stitch closed and tuck the lining inside.

MATERIALS

Purse
- 28 count gray linen, 13¾"x13¾" (35x35cm), plus a 7"x7" (18x18cm) piece for the backing
- Green lining fabric, two 7"x7" (18x18cm) pieces
- Ribbon, two 10" (25cm) pieces

We've chosen Kreinik braid to work all the gold details. It's thicker than embroidery thread, so stitch using just one strand for both the cross stitch and backstitch

	DMC	Anchor	Madeira
Cross stitch in three strands			
★	796	133	0913
♡	907	255	1410
#	913	204	1212
✕	3846	1090	1103
Cross stitch in one strand			
0	Kreinik (#8) fine braid 002		
Backstitch in one strand			
——	Kreinik (#8) fine braid 002 all details		

Make a... circular purse

Step 1

TRIM your stitching into a circle, leaving about ¾″ (1.5cm) of excess fabric beyond the stitched edge all the way around. Cut a second piece of gray linen for the backing and two pieces of green fabric for the lining to the same size and shape as your stitching.

Step 2

RIGHT sides in, pin your stitching and one of the green fabric pieces together, sandwiching a length of ribbon at the top. Sew, flush to the stitched edge, leaving an opening for turning. Repeat for the remaining fabric, linen and ribbon pieces.

Step 3

TURN each piece out, slip stitch the openings closed and press flat. Right sides out, pin the two sewn pieces together. Hand stitch together, only stitching through the two lining pieces. Work from top to bottom for each stitch, leaving an opening at the top.

You're just my TYPE

A vintage typewriter has to be one of the hottest design motifs right now, so help a friend smarten up their workspace with this retro-chic memo board

Designed by: Angela Poole
Stitch time: 60 hours

The more advanced our computers and other gadgets get these days, the more it seems we also value the simpler versions from the past. Fueled by hit TV series set in the workplaces of past decades – from *Mad Men* and *The Hour* to *Mr. Selfridge* and *Dancing on the Edge* – images of typewriters, twist-dial telephones, inkwells and other vintage office items are finding their way onto our modern-day stationery as well as homeware, fabrics and more. But you don't have to stick to authentic colors and details if you love this look. This retro typewriter design got a contemporary makeover with fresh blues and crisp whites, for you to make a memo board that will add style to anyone's workspace. Why not customize the design by making use of the paper space or the keys? Spell your message out!

Use the individual typewriter keys to personalize your stitching with a name or message

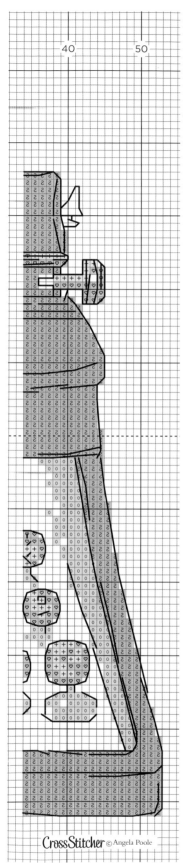

Anchor	DMC	Madeira
Cross stitch in two strands		
0 158	747	1101
S 167	3766	1111
+ 387	Ecru	2314
♥ 388	3033	1907
▲ 399	318	1802
◄► 401	413	1713
Backstitch in one strand		
—— 401	413	1713
all details		
French knots in one strand		
● 401	413	1713
all details		

MATERIALS

- 28 count white evenweave, 23¼"x23¼" (60x60cm)
- Grosgrain ribbon, 56" (140cm)
- Batting
- Square wooden frame
- White mount board
- Staple gun

Make a…
memo board

Step 1

STARTING with a basic square frame, cut a piece of foam core to exactly the same size as the outside edges. Attach it to the front using double-sided tape. This will create a flat surface.

Step 2

CUT TWO pieces of batting to the same size as the front of your frame and attach using double-sided tape. Trim your stitching so that you have enough excess to wrap around your frame.

Step 3

STRETCH your fabric tightly around to the back of your frame, securing with double-sided tape. Take care to fold the fabric neatly at each of the corners.

Step 4

STAPLE the fabric using a staple gun to keep it taut. Trim away any excess fabric. Secure any fabric edges with masking tape. Attach your grosgrain ribbon, securing on the back with a few staples.

make do
& MEND

Jump on the thrifty-chic bandwagon and stitch a friend these beautiful treats for her sewing room

Designed by: Felicity Hall
Stitch time: 4 hours each

Make a... **sewing box**

Step 1
ADD a couple of layers of batting to your box top, securing in place with some double-sided tape. Center your stitching on the box top. Stretch over the box once you're happy with the position, securing with double-sided tape.

Step 2
BE SURE to fold the evenweave carefully at the corners to create a crisp finish. For the base of the box, cut a piece of fabric that's large enough to cover the outside of the box, as well as the bottom and inside edges.

Step 3
BACK the entire piece with iron-on adhesive. Remove the paper backing. Fold the two side edges of your fabric under and press flat to create a hemmed effect. Begin adhering your fabric to the box, pulling taut as you go.

Step 4
ONCE you've finished securing the outsides, pull the excess to the inside and again carefully adhere with your iron. Finish by securing the excess fabric on the bottom, using a bit of fabric glue to further secure if necessary.

MATERIALS

Sewing box
- 26 count white evenweave, 15¾"x15¾" (40x40cm)
- Square cardboard box
- Navy blue fabric
- Iron-on adhesive
- Batting

Needle book

- 26 count raspberry evenweave, 7¼"x12¾" (18x32cm)
- Navy blue backing fabric, 4½"x11" (11x28cm)
- White felt, 2½"x8" (6.5x20cm)

	DMC	Anchor	Madeira
Cross stitch in three strands			
0	Ecru	387	2404
✕	445	288	0103
♥	608	330	0205
⋈	823	152	1008
☆	977	1002	2301
△	3806	062	0701
∫	3844	410	1103

CrossStitcher © Felicity Hall

Make a… **needle book**

Step 1

STITCH your design, ensuring you have at least 5 ½" (14cm) of space beyond the left hand stitched edge. Trim your stitching, leaving just ¾" (1.5cm) of space around the top, bottom and right-hand sides and 5 ½" (14cm) beyond the left-hand side.

Step 2

CUT a piece of navy blue fabric to the same size as your evenweave. Right sides together, machine stitch the two pieces together, leaving an opening for turning. Turn right sides out and slip stitch the opening closed.

Step 3

USE pinking shears to cut out a piece of white felt to about 2 ½"x8" (6.5x20cm). Attach to the inside of your needle book by working a running stitch through the center of the book. If you like you can add more than one layer of felt.

Giant pincushion
- 26 count orange evenweave, 10"x10" (25x25cm)
- Turquoise fabric, see step-by-step for sizing
- Stuffing

	DMC	Anchor	Madeira
Cross stitch in three strands			
0	Ecru	387	2404
×	445	288	0103
♥	608	330	0205
⋈	823	152	1008
☆	977	1002	2301
△	3806	062	0701
ς	3844	410	1103

CrossStitcher © Felicity Hall

Choose a brightly-colored backing fabric that matches one of the thread colors already in the design. Add some trims too if you like!

Make a... **giant pincushion**

Step 1

ONCE you've finished stitching, mark out a circle on the reverse of your evenweave. Trim your evenweave piece ¾" (2cm) beyond your drawn circle. Cut a piece of turquoise fabric for the bottom to the same size and shape.

Step 2

MEASURE around the circle shape with thread. Cut out the middle strip to ¾" (2cm) longer than the thread length and 3¼" (8cm) wide. With right sides in, pin and sew the strip to your stitching, along the drawn circle. Sew the ends of the strip closed.

Step 3

PIN and machine sew the bottom piece in place, using the same method. Leave an opening for turning. Turn right sides out and fill your pincushion with stuffing until it feels full and firm. Slip stitch the opening closed to finish.

KING OF COOL

Every modern gentleman should own a suitably cool
monochrome accessories case. Fact.

Designed by: Mr X Stitch **Design size:** 2½"x7¾" (6x18.5cm) **Stitch time:** 6 hours each

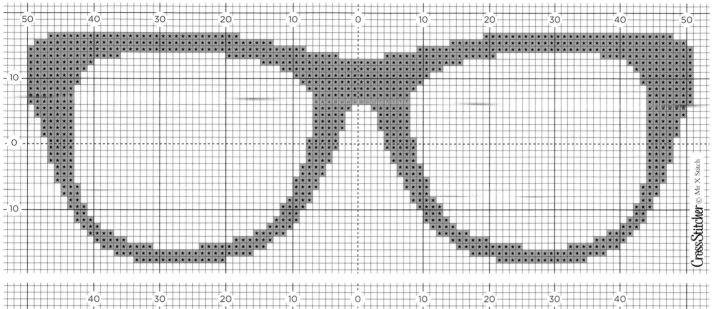

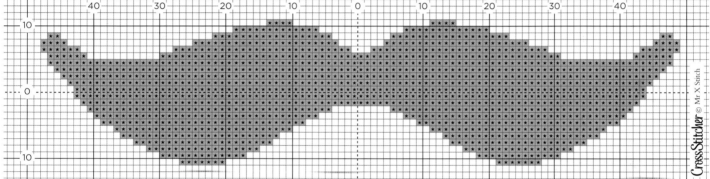

DMC	Anchor	Madeira
Cross stitch in three strands		
★ 310	403	2400

Make it easier to identify each evenweave hole by placing something dark beneath your fabric

Make a... **glasses case**

Step 1

STITCH your design in the center of your 9"x13 ½" (23x34cm) piece of rustic linen. Trim your stitching and a second piece of rustic linen to 4 ¾"x9 ½" (12x24cm). Then trim two cream fabric pieces for the lining and two pieces of batting to 4 ¾"x9 ½" (12x24cm) as well.

Step 2

LAY your stitching and a cream fabric piece right sides together, with a piece of batting on top. Machine sew through all three layers, along the top edge only. Repeat this step for the second pieces of rustic linen, cream fabric and batting.

Step 3

OPEN both sets of sewn pieces out and press the seams. Right sides in, sew around the outside edge, lining up the seams at the middle. Leave an opening for turning on the lining side. Turn right sides out, slip stitch closed and push the lining inside.

MATERIALS

- 28 count white evenweave, 21¾"x21¾" (55x55cm) for each
- White fabric, two 14¼"x14¼" (36x36cm) pieces for each cushion
- Stuffing
- Pom-pom trim, 1.5yds (1.5m) for each

Happy camper

Got a friend who lives for festivals, road trips and holidays? Help them cozy up their camping with this cool cushion duo

Designed by: Jane Prutton
Design size: 8"x9" (20x22.5cm)
Stitch time: 60 hours

ots of us dream of owning a traditional campervan and decking it out with handmade curtains and cushions (oh, to live the hippy-chic lifestyle), but for most of us it has to stay just a dream. You could make a dreamy friend extremely happy, however, with this pair of classic campervan cushions. These iconic vehicles are all over, adorning everything from tote bags to tea towels, and these cross stitched versions simply rock. Electric blue and punchy orange are authentic campervan shades, but you could easily change these to suit your friend's taste. Go wild with pom-pom trim for a cheery look, or for another gift idea finish in white box frames for a wall art look. Surf's up, dude.

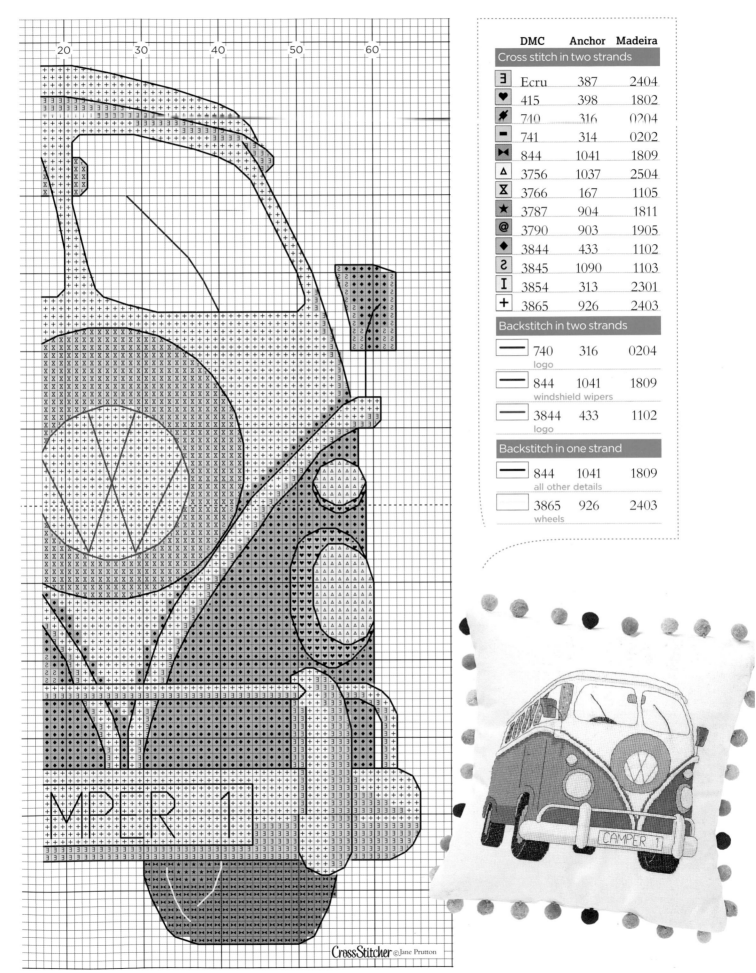

DMC	Anchor	Madeira
Cross stitch in two strands		
Ǝ Ecru	387	2404
♥ 415	398	1802
✦ 740	316	0204
− 741	314	0202
⋈ 844	1041	1809
△ 3756	1037	2504
X 3766	167	1105
★ 3787	904	1811
@ 3790	903	1905
◆ 3844	433	1102
S 3845	1090	1103
I 3854	313	2301
+ 3865	926	2403
Backstitch in two strands		
—— 740	316	0204
logo		
—— 844	1041	1809
windshield wipers		
—— 3844	433	1102
logo		
Backstitch in one strand		
—— 844	1041	1809
all other details		
☐ 3865	926	2403
wheels		

CrossStitcher ©Jane Prutton

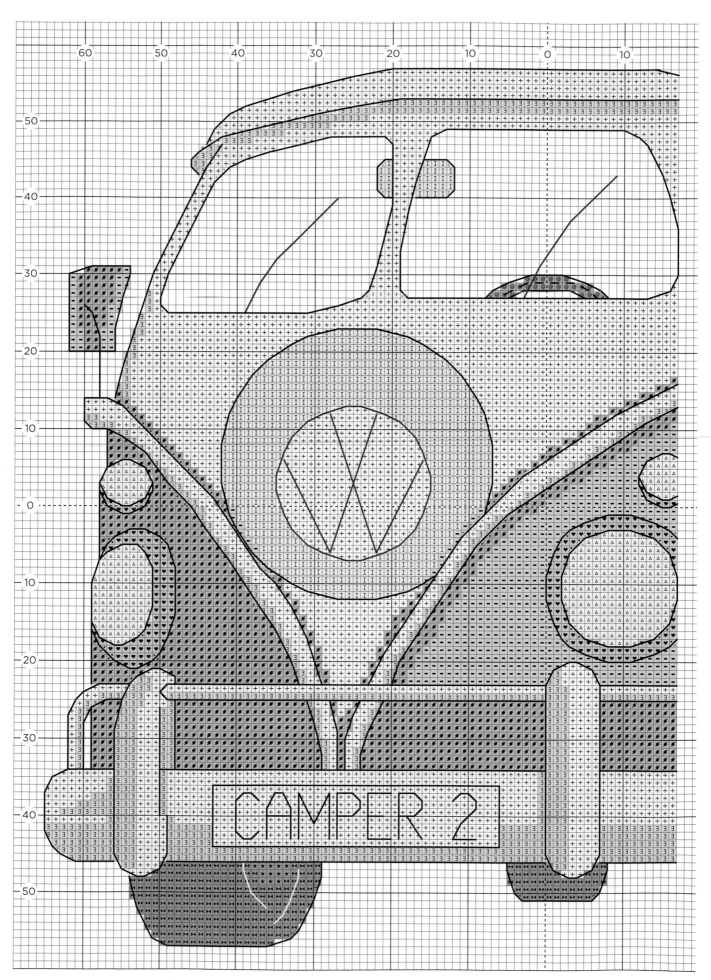

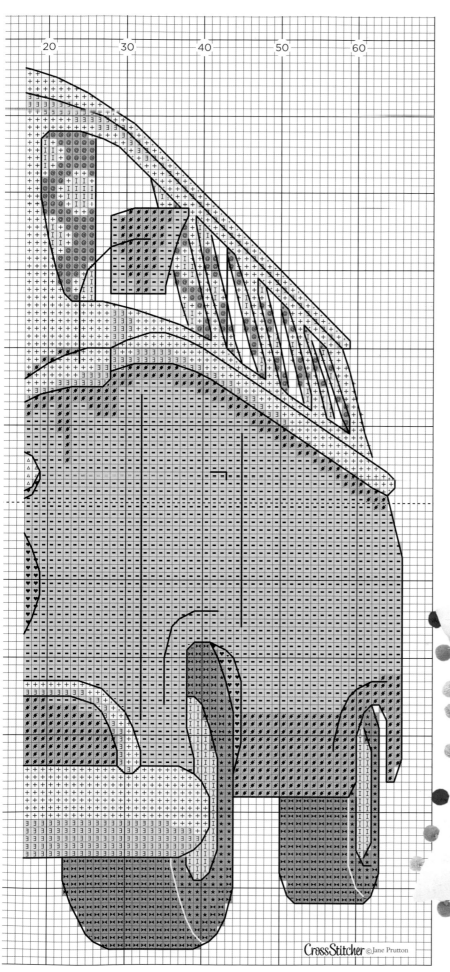

DMC	Anchor	Madeira
Cross stitch in two strands		
Ǝ Ecru	387	2404
♥ 415	398	1802
✖ 740	316	0204
▬ 741	314	0202
▶◀ 844	1041	1809
△ 3756	1037	2504
X 3766	167	1105
★ 3787	904	1811
@ 3790	903	1905
◆ 3844	433	1102
ƨ 3845	1090	1103
I 3854	313	2301
+ 3865	926	2403
Backstitch in two strands		
— 740 logo	316	0204
— 844 windshield wipers	1041	1809
— 3844 logo	433	1102
Backstitch in one strand		
— 844 all other details	1041	1809
— 3865 wheels	926	2403

CrossStitcher ©Jane Prutton

Designer Cross Stitch Projects   **69**

Make a... cushion

Step 1

ONCE you've finished stitching, trim your stitching and two pieces of white fabric to measure 14 ¼"x14 ¼" (36x36cm). Pin and hand tack your pom-pom trim in place on the cushion front.

Step 2

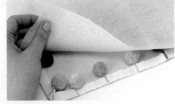

BACK your stitching with one of the pieces of white fabric. Right sides in, place your second fabric piece over your stitching. Using a machine zipper foot, stitch around, as close to the edge of the trim as possible. Leave an opening for turning, turn, fill with stuffing and slip stitch the opening closed.

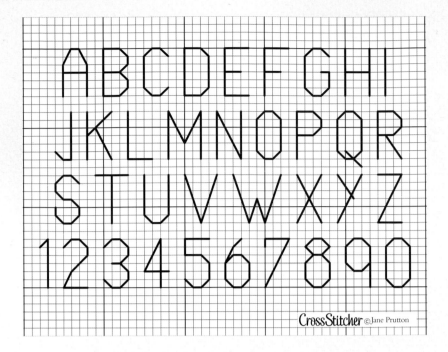

ABCDEFGHI
JKLMNOPQR
STUVWXYZ
1234567890

CrossStitcher ©Jane Prutton

Use this alphabet chart to personalize the number plates to suit yourself or your recipient

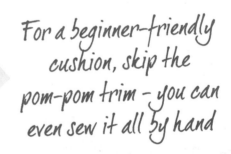

For a beginner-friendly cushion, skip the pom-pom trim - you can even sew it all by hand

Mellow *yellow*

Inject some sunshine into a friend's life with this cheerful design for a bag and a covered notebook

Designed by: Lucie Heaton
Design size: 9"x9¼" (22.5x23.5cm)
Stitch time: 18 hours

DMC	Anchor	Madeira
Cross stitch in two strands		
~ 727	293	0110
✕ 743	305	0113
★ 947	330	0205
♡ 972	298	0107
Backstitch in two strands		
—— 900	333	0208
'you are my' lettering		
—— 947	330	0205
'you are my' lettering		
Backstitch in one strand		
—— 900	333	0208
'sunshine' lettering		
—— 947	330	0205
suns, 'sunshine' lettering		

Make a...
covered notebook
Step 1

TRIM your stitching to 10 ¾" (27cm) tall and 10" (25cm) wide, leaving just 1 ½" (4cm) beyond the left hand stitched edge. Back your stitching with a piece of white fabric that's exactly the same size. If you are not using a 9"x17 ½" (22.5x44cm) A5 notebook, adjust the size to suit.

Step 2

MACHINE stitch a 10 ¾"x10 ¾" (27x27cm) piece of fabric to the left side of your stitching, then open out and press the seam flat. Cut a second piece of fabric to the same size as your sewn piece. Right sides in, pin and machine sew the two pieces together, leaving an opening for turning.

Step 3

TURN right sides out and slip stitch the opening closed. Fold the right and left hand sides toward the middle, creating pockets. Hand-sew the top and bottom of each pocket, only sewing through the lining.

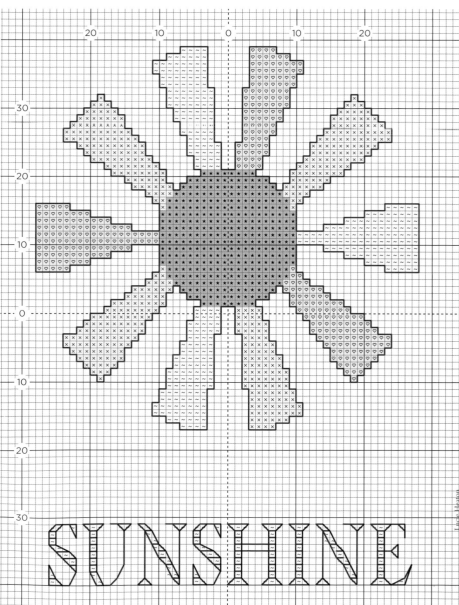

Lucie Heaton

MATERIALS

Notebook
- 28 count white evenweave, 13¾"x13¾" (35x35cm)
- Patterned fabric, see step-by-step for sizing
- White fabric, see step-by-step for sizing
- Notebook

DMC	Anchor	Madeira
Cross stitch in two strands		
~ 727	293	0110
✕ 743	305	0113
★ 947	330	0205
♥ 972	298	0107
Backstitch in two strands		
900	333	0208
'you are my' lettering		
947	330	0205
'you are my' lettering		
Backstitch in one strand		
900	333	0208
'sunshine' lettering		
947	330	0205
suns, 'sunshine' lettering		

MATERIALS

Bag
- 28 count white evenweave, 19¾"x19¾" (50x50cm)
- Patterned fabric, see step-by-step for sizing
- White fabric, see step-by-step for sizing

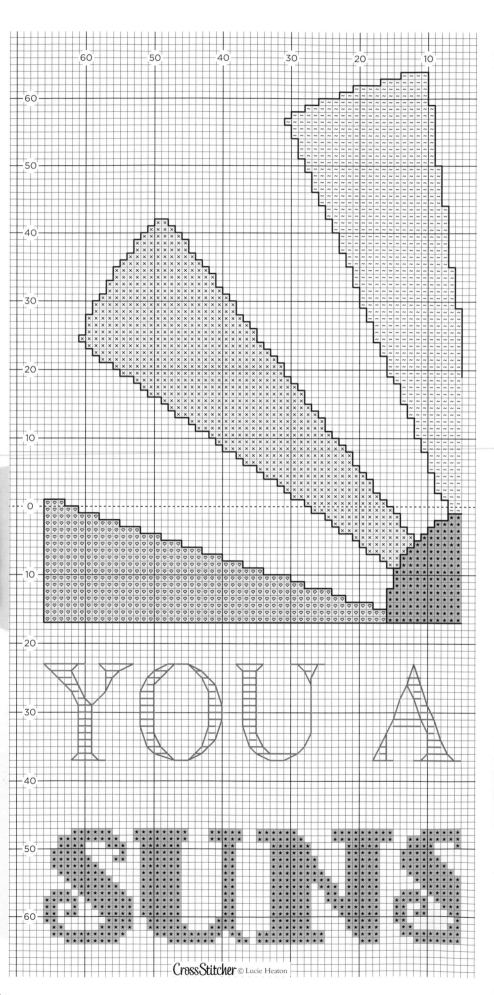

CrossStitcher © Lucie Heaton

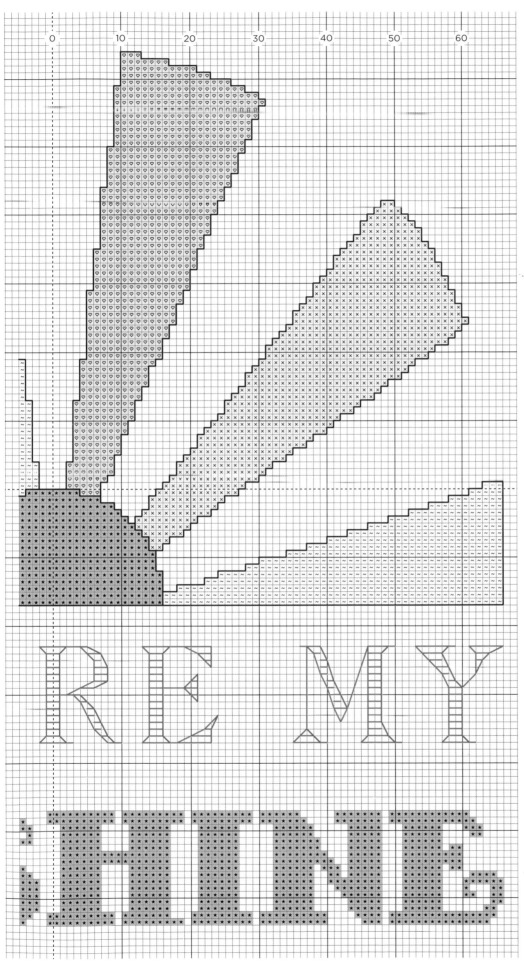

Turn to page 80 for a step-by-step guide to making a bag from your stitched evenweave plus other fabric

BE A GOOD
sport

Retro colors and bold motifs make these designs an eye-catching alternative to boring old gym bags

Designed by: Felicity Hall
Design size: 8"x9½" (20x24cm)
Stitch time: 35 hours

Get set – go! Since the London Olympics, everyone's crazy for sporty motifs, and what better way to join in the fun than with a pair of retro designs for gym bags? Here are two different looks for you to choose from – a drawstring bag and a shopping-style tote. Your kids, partner or anyone who regularly pulls their sneakers on to get active would love one of these bags to make them stand out from the crowd in the changing room!

MATERIALS

Drawstring bag

- 28 count white evenweave, 17¾"x17¾" (45x45cm)
- Green fabric, see step-by-step for sizing
- White fabric, see step-by-step for sizing
- Cream cord, 1yd (1m)

	DMC	Anchor	Madeira		DMC	Anchor	Madeira
Cross stitch in two strands				**Cross stitch in two strands**			
~	307	289	0104	X	972	298	0107
◄►	310	403	2400	▲	3843	1089	1103
♥	349	013	0212	**Backstitch in one strand**			
0	743	305	0113	—	310	403	2400
★	911	205	1214			all details	

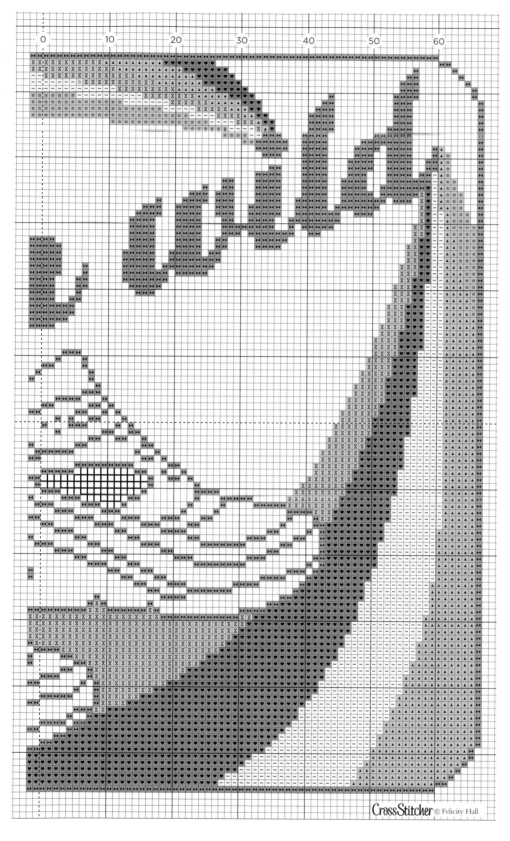

CrossStitcher © Felicity Hall

Make a...
drawstring bag

Step 1

TRIM your stitching to 12 ¾″ (32cm) wide and 11″ (28cm) tall. Back with a piece of white fabric. Sew a 12 ¾″x8″ (32x20cm) piece of fabric along the top of your stitching. Cut a second piece of fabric to the same size as your sewn piece. Fold and pin along the right and left sides of each piece and sew in place.

Step 2

MAKE about a 1 ½″ (4cm) fold from the top edge of each fabric piece to the reverse. Pin and sew in place to create a channel.

Step 3

WITH the right sides facing in, pin and sew along the sides and bottom of the bag. Make sure you only sew below the drawstring channels you created in step 2. Turn your bag right side out. Thread your cord through the channels and tighten to finish.

We've left the sneakers plain white, but you could personalize them to match the recipient's team or school colors

Designer Cross Stitch Projects   **79**

Make a...
shopping bag

Step 1

TRIM your stitching to 11 ½"x12 ¾" (29x32cm). Back your stitching with a piece of white fabric that's exactly the same size. Right sides in, machine stitch a 5 ¼"x12 ¾" (13x32cm) strip of fabric along the top edge of your stitching, sewing through both fabric layers.

Step 2

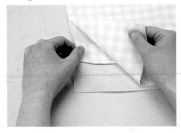

CUT two lining pieces and a backing piece to the same size as your sewn front piece. To create the handles, stitch two 2 ½"x21 ¾" (6x55cm) fabric strips together, right sides in. Turn out, press and repeat for the other handle. Pin and machine sew your stitched piece and one lining piece together, sandwiching one of your handles between the layers. Repeat for the backing piece, second lining piece and second handle.

Step 3

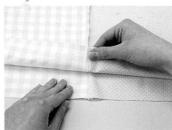

OPEN both pieces out and pin together, right sides in, lining up the seams at the middle. Sew around, leaving an opening for turning. Turn, slip stitch closed and tuck the lining inside.

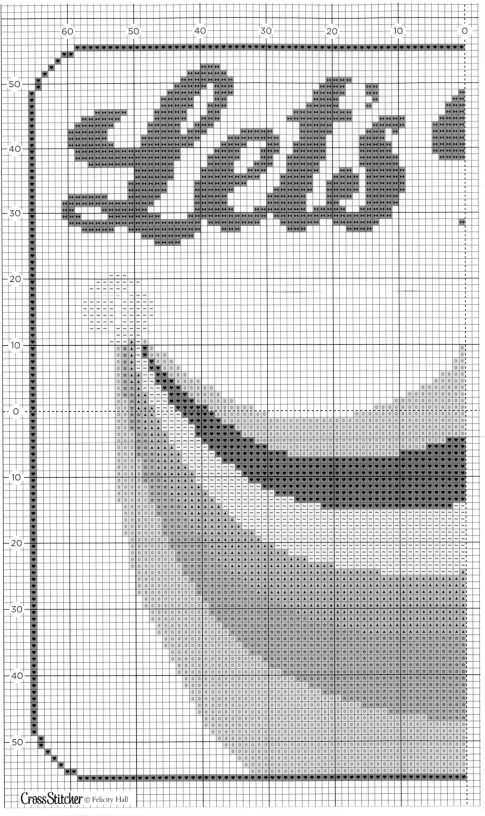

CrossStitcher © Felicity Hall

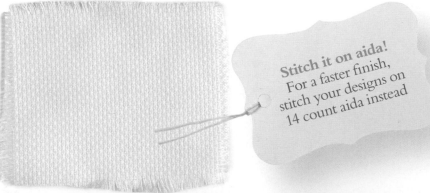

Stitch it on aida! For a faster finish, stitch your designs on 14 count aida instead

A few sparkling seed beads in matching shades to the stripes would really give the rainbow motif some dazzle!

Shopping bag
- 28 count white evenweave, 17¾"x17¾" (45x45cm)
- Ochre fabric, see step-by-step for sizing
- White fabric, see step-by-step for sizing

	DMC	Anchor	Madeira		DMC	Anchor	Madeira
Cross stitch in two strands				**Cross stitch in two strands**			
~	307	289	0104	X	972	298	0107
⋈	310	403	2400	▲	3843	1089	1103
♥	349	013	0212	**Backstitch in one strand**			
0	743	305	0113	—	310	403	2400
★	911	205	1214		all details		

Homestyle

Cross stitch looks amazing anywhere, so fill your home with the color and character of these gorgeous pictures, accessories and cushions.

The Butterfly effect

Capture your own botanical beauty with this irresistible wall hanging that's guaranteed to become the center of attention

The large, brightly colored wings of these charming creatures are symbolic signs of beauty, and there's no denying this project hits the spot as a feature piece. Forget dusty display cabinets and gloomy scientific drawings, because this vibrant butterfly was designed to shine! With its vintage-lace-inspired border and stunning bluebottle shades, you'll find it hard to resist showing this one off.

Designed by: Felicity Hall
Stitch time: 85 hours
Finished size: 11"x14¼" (28x36cm)

MATERIALS

- 25 count putty evenweave, 22½"x25¾" (57x65cm)
- Cream backing fabric, 17¾"x21" (45x53cm)
- Metal chain, 1yd (1m)
- White paint
- Wooden dowel, two 20" (50cm) lengths

Turn to page 89 to learn how to transform your stitching into a wall hanging

DMC	Anchor	Madeira
Cross stitch in three strands		
O B5200	001	2401
@ 322	978	1004
★ 797	132	0912
◇ 964	185	1112
△ 3753	1031	1001
♥ 3808	1068	2507
⌇ 3845	433	1103
Ⅎ 3849	1070	1109
Backstitch in two strands		
▬ 3808	1068	2507
all details		

CrossStitcher © Felicity Hall

NEON BRIGHTS

Indulge in the current flamingo trend with
an electric hanger that's sure to become
a focal point. Mojito, anyone?

Electric neon hues and exotic retro prints are everywhere right now. The classic pink flamingo is an icon of American kitsch, but rather than installing a flock across your lawn, how about stitching up this bright beauty instead? The tropical flowers and palm trees scream 1950s Americana, and are sure to cheer up any plain wall. It'd look great hung above a retro cocktail bar, so you can wow your guests while you serve them their favorite beverages.

	DMC	Anchor	Madeira
Cross stitch in three strands			
0	Ecru	387	2404
✗	307	290	0104
▶◀	310	403	2400
♥	326	059	0508
~	445	288	0103
Ǝ	606	334	0209
★	905	257	1412
✕	907	255	1410
▲	972	298	0107
◆	995	410	1102
⌒	996	433	1103
✩	3705	035	0410
♡	3706	033	0408
◇	3824	008	2503

MATERIALS

- 25 count pale blue evenweave, 19¾"x23¾" (50x60cm)
- Pale blue backing fabric, 12"x17½" (30x44cm)
- Wooden dowel, 12" (30cm)
- Turquoise cord, 30" (75cm)
- Pom-pom trim, 12" (26cm)

Make a... **hanging picture**

Step 1
TRIM your stitching to just ¾" (1.5cm) beyond the bottom and side stitched edges. Leave about 3¼" (8cm) beyond the top stitched edge. Cut a piece of pale blue backing fabric to the same size. With right sides in, machine sew the sides and bottom, sandwiching your length of pom-pom trim along the bottom edge and leaving the top edge open.

Step 2
TURN right sides out, fold the top edges in and machine stitch over to secure. Fold the unstitched excess fabric along the top edge to the reverse, creating a channel for the dowel. Secure with tacking stitches. Slide in your dowel and tie cord to each end to finish.

Designed by: Felicity Hall Design size: 10¾"x13½" (27x34cm)
Stitch time: 94 hours

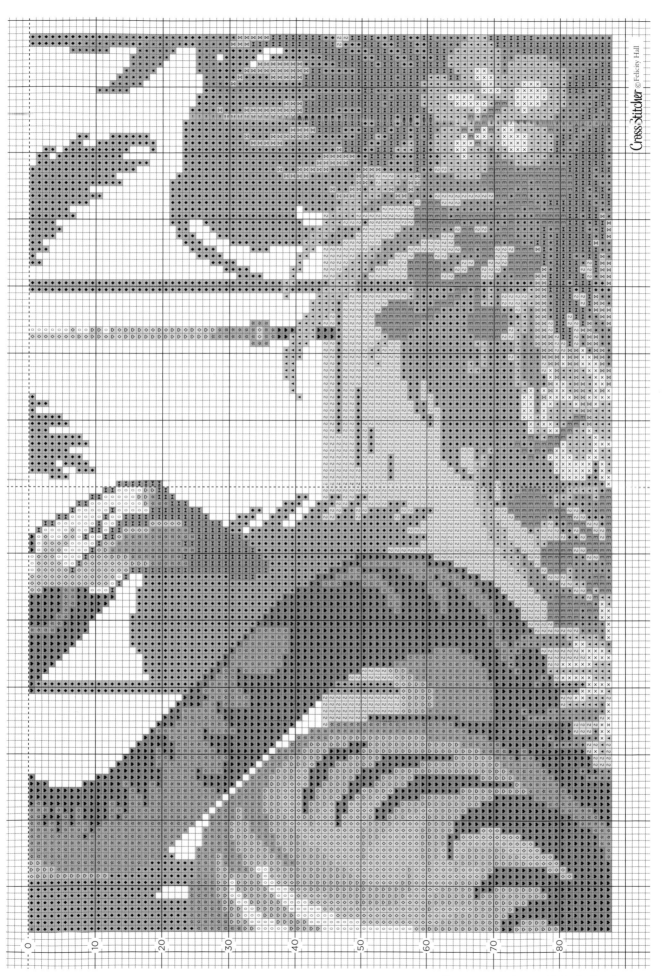

Black Magic

For all those style-conscious interior design fanatics out there, here's a frame that's picture perfect for your latest look

Designed by: Lesley Teare
Design size: 7"x8¼" (18x21cm)
Stitch time: 22 hours

MATERIALS

- 28 count rustic linen, 13¾"x16½" (35x42cm)
- Batting, two 7½"x8¾" (19x22cm) pieces
- White mount board, 7½"x8¾" (19x22cm)
- Black ribbon, 16" (40cm) (optional)
- Two push pins (optional)

Make a...
padded frame

Step 1

CUT a piece of white mount board to 7 ½"x8 ¾" (19x22cm). Cut two pieces of batting to the same size. Attach the first piece of batting to your board using a thin layer of fabric glue. Place the second piece on top – you don't need to secure this piece.

Step 2

ADD diagonal stitches in each corner of your frame, which will hold your picture in place. Press your stitching until smooth and trim to 11"x12 ¼" (28x31cm). Center your stitching over the batting-covered board. Pull the edges to the reverse and secure with double-sided tape, just as you would if you were framing a traditional stitched picture.

Step 3

CAREFULLY fold the fabric at the corners, keeping them as neat as possible. Secure excess fabric at the corners with a glue gun or fabric glue if necessary. Add masking tape over the raw edges for a neat finish. Attach ribbon at the top, securing with a push pin at each corner.

Stitch it on aida!
For a faster finish, try 14 count rustic aida instead

Make four extra secure stitches in each of the four corners of your frame so you can slip in a photo

DMC	Anchor	Madeira
Cross stitch in three strands		
310	403	2400

CrossStitcher © Lesley Teare

Shocking color

Any sofa that has this spectacular cushion sitting on it wins style points galore – and this one has a funky message too

◇◇◇◇◇◇◇◇◇◇◇◇◇◇◇◇◇◇◇◇

Designed by: Emily Peacock Stitch time: 85 hours

MATERIALS

- 28 count putty evenweave, 19"x31½" (48x80cm)
- Backing fabric, 13¾"x26" (35x66cm)
- Pom-pom trim, 2yds (2m)
- Stuffing

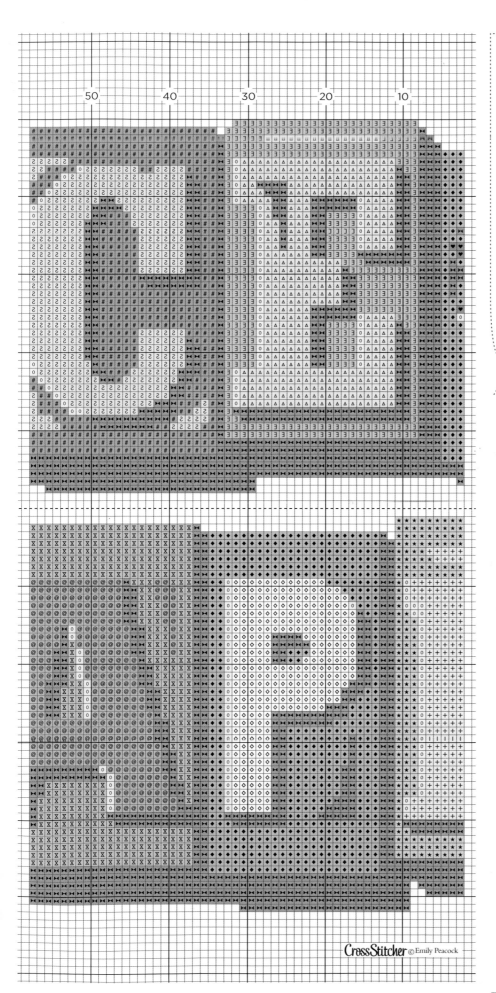

	DMC	Anchor	Madeira
Cross stitch in three strands			
2	166	279	1308
◇	445	288	0103
#	553	098	0712
@	602	057	0702
♡	726	295	0109
X	741	304	0203
◆	798	146	0911
♥	817	013	0211
+	827	160	1002
⋈	839	1086	1913
★	906	256	1411
△	3716	025	0606
Ǝ	3845	433	1103
0	3865	926	2403

Turn to page 70 for a step-by-step guide to making up your cushion with a pom-pom fringe

CrossStitcher ©Emily Peacock

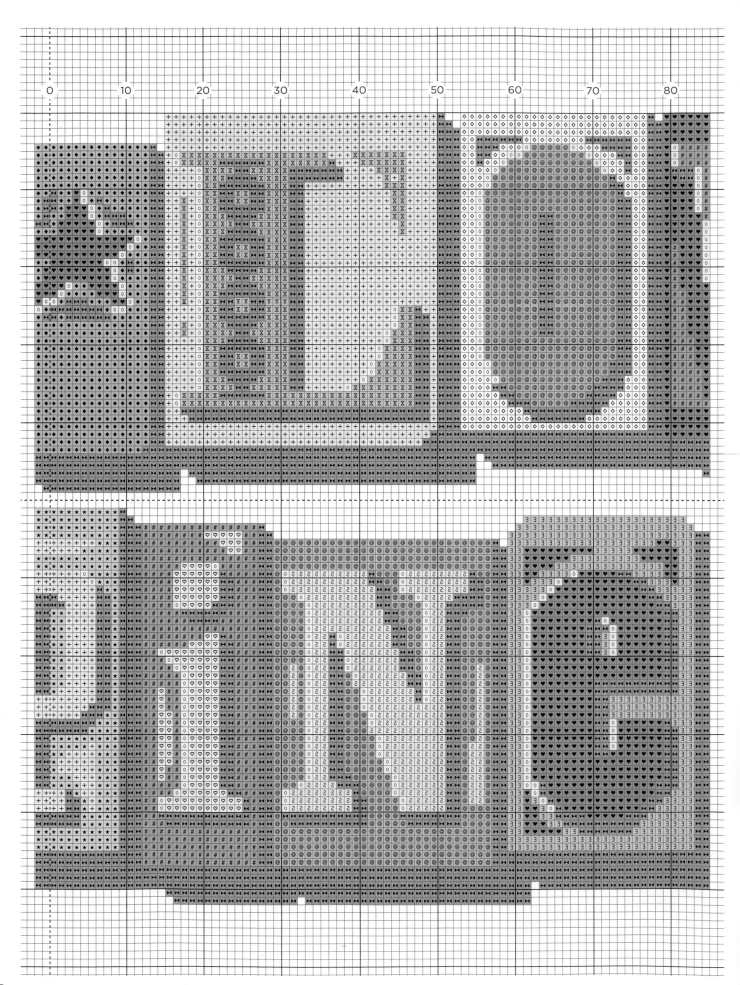

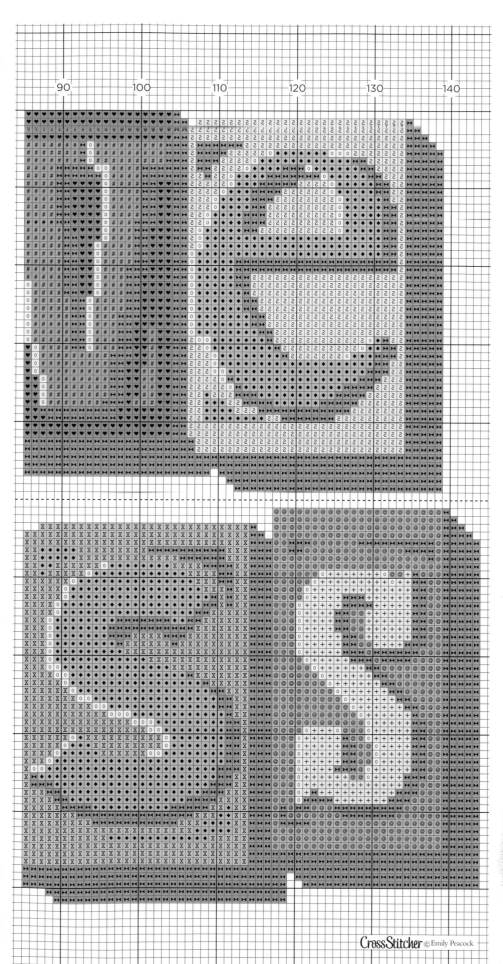

	DMC	Anchor	Madeira
Cross stitch in three strands			
𝟤	166	279	1308
◇	445	288	0103
#	553	098	0712
@	602	057	0702
♡	726	295	0109
X	741	304	0203
◆	798	146	0911
♥	817	013	0211
+	827	160	1002
◄►	839	1086	1913
★	906	256	1411
△	3716	025	0606
Ǝ	3845	433	1103
0	3865	926	2403

If you're feeling impatient, why not stitch just one of the three words on its own?

Stitch it on aida!
If you'd rather stitch on aida, go for 14 count rustic aida instead

CrossStitcher © Emily Peacock

MATERIALS

- 28 count rustic linen, 21¼"x23"
  (54x58cm) piece, two 2½"x23¾"
  (6x60cm) strips
- Red polka dot fabric, 15"x17"
  (38x43cm) piece, 3¼"x15"
  (8x38cm) strip, two
  2½"x23¾" (6x60cm) strips
- Cream lining fabric, two
  15"x17" (38x43cm) pieces

Flower
Power

Go bright and bold with an eye-catching bloom that's sure to rival even the most vibrant cushions in home dec stores

Designed by: Lesley Teare
Design size: 15¾"x15¾" (40x40cm)
Stitch time: 136 hours

Why settle for subtle pastel shades when there's all this luscious evenweave to play with? This psychedelic flower cushion is a much more attention-grabbing alternative and will be way more fun to stitch too! Be brave and create a colorful centerpiece for your home that really has the "WOW" factor.

Make a... **circular cushion**

Step 1

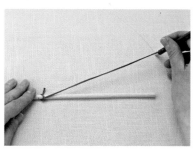

Step 2

Step 3

ONCE you've finished stitching, trace a circle on the reverse that's approximately 18" (45cm) across. Use a knitting needle, thread and pencil (as shown) to draw a circle. Trim your stitching and a piece of patterned fabric to ¾" (1.5cm) beyond the circle.

RIGHT sides in, pin and machine stitch the two pieces together, leaving an opening for turning. Turn right sides out and fill firmly with stuffing. You might be surprised by how much stuffing you'll need! Slip stitch closed.

COVER a 1½" (38mm) self-cover button with the same patterned fabric you used for the backing. Attach the button, sewing through the cushion from the front to the back several times to create a dent in the center of the cushion on both sides.

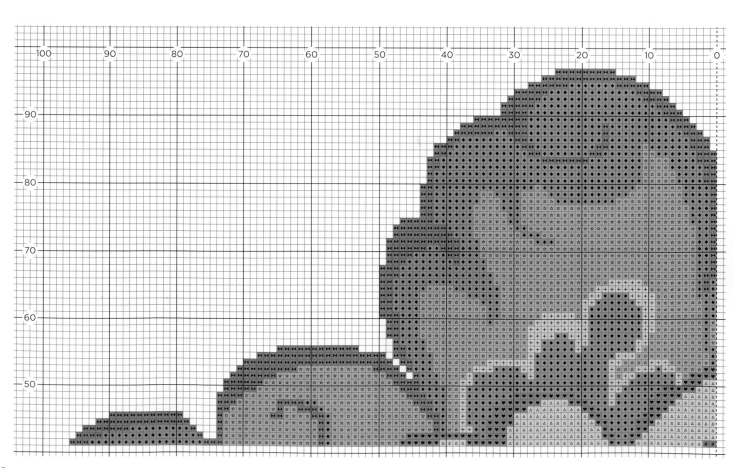

	DMC	Anchor	Madeira
Cross stitch in three strands			
◆	309	042	0508
~	725	305	0108
⋈	815	044	0513
ƨ	900	333	0208
♡	907	255	1410
♥	915	1029	0705
#	917	089	0706
0	972	298	0107
⊠	3607	087	0708
△	3608	086	0709
☆	3831	039	0507
+	3833	1023	0609
Ǝ	3853	1003	0311

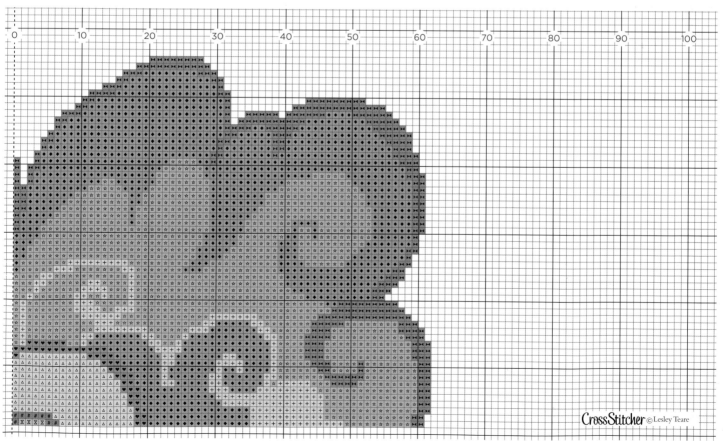

CrossStitcher © Lesley Teare

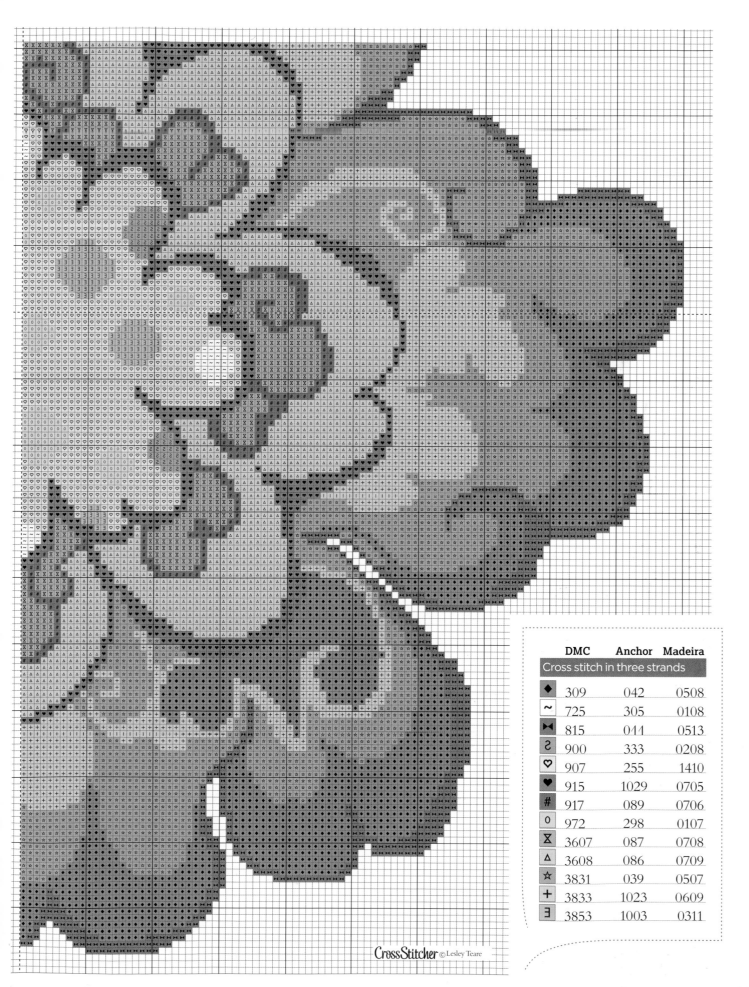

DMC	Anchor	Madeira
Cross stitch in three strands		
♦ 309	042	0508
~ 725	305	0108
⋈ 815	044	0513
S 900	333	0208
♡ 907	255	1410
♥ 915	1029	0705
# 917	089	0706
O 972	298	0107
⊠ 3607	087	0708
△ 3608	086	0709
☆ 3831	039	0507
+ 3833	1023	0609
Ǝ 3853	1003	0311

CrossStitcher © Lesley Teare

CARNIVAL QUEEN

Step right up! Recreate the fun of the fairground with this vintage poster in tasty candy brights

Designed by: Felicity Hall
Design size: 9¼"x9¾" (23.5x24.5cm)
Stitch time: 55 hours

We're all familiar with the war-time "Keep Calm" prints that seized our imagination and went viral, but beyond that there's an ever-growing passion for all kinds of vintage posters. Why do we love them? Maybe it's because the evocative designs and colors of past decades tap into our childhood memories and remind us of our cultural heritage – or maybe it's simply because they look so stylish! "I'm often inspired by items that I find at antiques fairs or in junk shops and charity shops," says this carnival poster's designer, Felicity Hall. "Retro posters are favorites, as well as plates and ornaments." Let the candy-floss and bubblegum colors of Felicity's design remind you of fairground fun as you stitch!

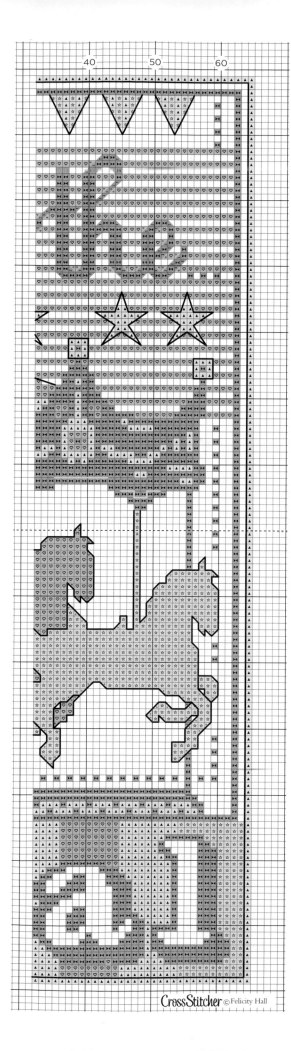

The 1950s candy colors of this carnival poster make for a tasty stitching treat!

	DMC	Anchor	Madeira
Cross stitch in two strands			
♥	894	026	0408
★	959	186	1113
⋈	3799	236	1713
▲	3820	306	2509
Backstitch in one strand			
——	310	403	2400
all other details			
——	3820	306	2509
merry-go-round, banner, star			

MATERIALS

- 28 count white evenweave, 19¾"x19¾" (50x50cm)
- Iron-on interfacing (optional)

More Great Books from Design Originals

Ultimate Cross Stitch Projects
ISBN 978-1-57421-444-4 **$19.99**
DO5417

Irresistible Gifts to Cross Stitch
ISBN 978-1-57421-445-1 **$19.99**
DO5416

Cross Stitched Cards for Special Occasions
ISBN 978-1-57421-376-8 **$9.99**
DO3500

Cross Stitched Cards for the Holidays
ISBN 978-1-57421-380-5 **$9.99**
DO3503

Handmade for Christmas
ISBN 978-1-57421-508-3 **$14.99**
DO5429

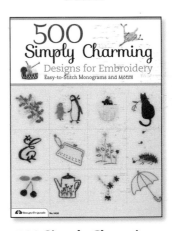

500 Simply Charming Designs for Embroidery
ISBN 978-1-57421-509-0 **$14.99**
DO5430

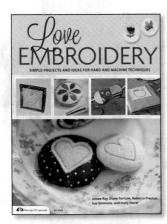

Love Embroidery
ISBN 978-1-57421-612-7 **$17.99**
DO5302

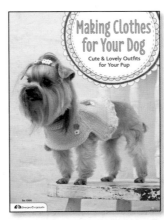

Making Clothes for Your Dog
ISBN 978-1-57421-610-3 **$19.99**
DO5300

Sewing Pretty Little Things
ISBN 978-1-57421-611-0 **$19.99**
DO5301